BREAKFAST AND
BRUNCHES

Licensed and produced by:

DIRECT SOURCE
SPECIAL PRODUCTS INC.

©℗1999 DIRECT SOURCE SPECIAL PRODUCTS INC.
Canada: P.O. Box 361,
Victoria Station, Westmount,
Quebec, Canada
H3Z 2V8
U.S.: P.O. Box 2189,
609 New York Road, Plattsburgh,
New York, 12903

Recipes and photos courtesy of:
Les Éditions Multi-Concept Inc.

Printed in Canada

ISBN# 1-896306-47-0

APPETIZERS 6

SIDE DISHES 22

EGG DISHES 38

SANDWICHES, CROISSANTS AND BAGELS 54

MAIN DISHES 66

SWEET DELIGHTS 80

PARTRIDGE SOUP WITH MUSHROOMS

4 SERVINGS

Preparation Time: 20 minutes
Cooking Time: 1 hour

4 tsp	(20 ml) butter
1/2 cup	(125 ml) chopped onions
1/2 cup	(125 ml) diced celery
1/2 cup	(125 ml) diced carrots
2	partridges, each cut into 4 pieces
1	bay leaf
1	sprig of thyme
1	sprig of parsley
1 tsp	(5 ml) dried savory
5 cups	(1.25 L) beef stock
1 1/2 cups	(375 ml) wild mushrooms (chanterelles, morels or oyster mushrooms) salt and pepper, to taste
1/2 cup	(125 ml) sherry
1	flaky pastry
1	medium egg, beaten with 2 tbsp (25 ml) milk

In a large pot, melt 2 tsp (10 ml) of butter and brown the onions, celery, carrots and the pieces of partridge.

Add the bay leaf, thyme, parsley, savory and beef stock. Let simmer over low heat for 30 to 35 minutes. Skim off the fat while cooking.

Debone and mince the partridge. Return to the stock and keep warm.

In a frying pan, sauté the mushrooms in 2 tsp (10 ml) of butter, add the sherry and season to taste. Incorporate to the partridge stock.

Preheat the oven to 350°F (180°C). On a lightly floured surface, cut 4 in (10 cm) rounds of the flaky pastry. Place on a cookie sheet and lightly poke the dough with a fork. Brush with the beaten eggs. Bake for 12 to 15 minutes.

Serve hot with the pastry on top.

TOULOUSE SALAD

4 SERVINGS

Preparation Time: 5 minutes
Cooking Time: 15 minutes

2 tsp	(10 ml) vegetable oil
6 to 8	sausages
8	lettuce leaves, of choice
8	slices of bread, lightly toasted and cut into triangles
1 cup	(250 ml) Mexican salsa fine herbs, to taste

In a pot of boiling water, blanch the sausages for 5 minutes over low heat. Once cooled, slice them lengthwise, in two.

In a pan, heat the oil and cook the sausages for 3 to 4 minutes on each side until golden.

Line the plates with lettuce, add the bread, sausages and Mexican salsa. Garnish with fine herbs.

CRAZY LITTLE SALAD

4 SERVINGS

Preparation Time: 10 minutes
Cooking Time: none

2 oz	(60 g) sun dried tomatoes
1	egg yolk
1 tsp	(5 ml) Dijon mustard
1/4 cup	(50 ml) balsamic vinegar
1/2 cup	(125 ml) olive oil
1/2 cup	(125 ml) vegetable oil
1/4 cup	(50 ml) warm water
	salt and pepper, to taste
6 cups	(1.5 L) mixed greens (endives, radicchio, watercress, etc.)

GARNISH

chopped chives
edible flowers (optional)

Soak the sundried tomatoes in warm water for 1 hour. Drain and purée in a food processor. Add the egg yolks, mustard and balsamic vinegar. Season and mix well. Add the oils and thin the vinaigrette with a little of the warm water. Adjust the seasoning as desired. Line the four plates with the mixed greens and dress with vinaigrette. Garnish with chopped chives and edible flowers.

PARTRIDGE AND VEAL TERRINE

10 SERVINGS

Preparation Time: 25 minutes
Cooking Time: 1 hour

1	veal tongue
1	partridge
1 lb	(500 g) veal shoulder, deboned
1/2 lb	(250 g) bacon
2	medium eggs
1 tbsp	(15 ml) finely chopped, fresh thyme
2 tbsp	(25 ml) finely chopped, fresh marjoram
2 tbsp	(25 ml) finely chopped, fresh parsley
1	finely chopped bay leaf
30	whole pistachios or walnuts
1 cup	(250 ml) dry white wine
2 tbsp	(25 ml) brandy or cognac
	salt and pepper, to taste

Soak the veal tongue in cold water for approximately 1 hour, changing the water regularly. In a pot, bring water to a boil and cook the veal tongue for 15 minutes, remove and set aside.

Debone the partridge and remove the skin. With a cleaver, mince the partridge legs, the pork and half of the bacon. Cut the partridge breasts and the veal tongue into thin strips; set aside.

Preheat the oven to 375°F (190°C). In a bowl, mix together the minced meat, eggs, fine herbs, bay leaf, pistachios, white wine and brandy; season.

In a terrine, alternately layer the minced meat preparation and strips of partridge and veal. Sprinkle the remaining bacon over top. Place the terrine in a large pan filled with sufficient water to surround the mold and bake for approximately 1 hour. Cool and let set for 24 hours in the refrigerator.

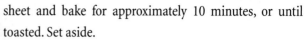
CITRUS SPINACH AND WATERCRESS SALAD

4 SERVINGS

Preparation Time: 15 minutes
Cooking Time: none

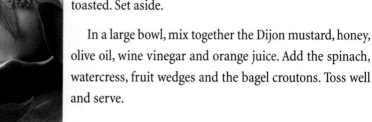

2	bagels, cubed
1 tsp	(5 ml) Dijon mustard
1/2 tsp	(2 ml) honey
1/3 cup	(75 ml) olive oil
2 tbsp	(25 ml) cider or wine vinegar
1/4 cup	(50 ml) orange juice
1	bag of spinach, washed and dried
2 cups	(500 ml) watercress
1	grapefruit, peeled and cut into wedges
2	oranges, peeled and cut into wedges
1	lemon or lime, peeled and cut into wedges

Preheat the oven to 350°F (180°C). Spread the bagel cubes on a cookie sheet and bake for approximately 10 minutes, or until toasted. Set aside.

In a large bowl, mix together the Dijon mustard, honey, olive oil, wine vinegar and orange juice. Add the spinach, watercress, fruit wedges and the bagel croutons. Toss well and serve.

MINCED PORK WITH MUSTARD SAUCE

10 TO 15 SERVINGS

Preparation Time: 40 minutes
Cooking Time: 2 hours 20 minutes

8 lb	(4 kg) pork knuckles
1 1/2 cups	(375 ml) dry white wine
4 cups	(1 L) water
2	medium onions, coarsely chopped
2	garlic cloves, minced
2	carrots, cut into pieces
2	stalks of celery, cut into pieces
2 tbsp	(25 ml) chopped, fresh rosemary
1 tbsp	(15 ml) unflavored gelatin
1/3 cup	(75 ml) lemon juice
1/2 cup	(125 ml) white wine vinegar
	salt and pepper, to taste

MUSTARD SAUCE

3/4 cup	(175 ml) Dijonnaise mustard
2 tbsp	(25 ml) old fashioned grainy mustard
2 tbsp	(25 ml) dry white wine
2 tbsp	(25 ml) lemon juice
1 tbsp	(25 ml) corn oil

In a large pot, combine the pork knuckles, white wine, water, onions, garlic, carrots, celery and rosemary. Bring slowly to a boil, while skimming fat from the top. Cover, lower the heat, and let simmer for 2 hours or until the meat detaches from the knuckles.

Remove the pork knuckles from the pot. Pour the stock through a strainer or cheesecloth and throw away the vegetables. Return the stock to the pot, bring to a boil and let reduce by one half.

Remove from the stove and add the gelatin; mix well until it dissolves. Add the lemon juice and the white wine vinegar. Season and let cool; set aside.

Meanwhile, remove the remaining meat from the pork knuckles, and discard the bones. Mince the meat and place in a terrine mold lined with plastic wrap. Pour in the cooled bouillon (just enough to cover the meat). Cover with plastic wrap and refrigerate for at least 6 hours or until well set.

Prepare the mustard sauce in a bowl by mixing together the Dijonnaise mustard, the grainy mustard, white wine, lemon juice and oil. Remove the minced pork from the mold and place on a serving plate. Serve with the mustard sauce.

MELON, CRAB AND SPINACH SALAD

4 SERVINGS
Preparation Time: 20 minutes
Cooking Time: none

1	honeydew melon, cut in half and seeded
1	cantaloupe, cut in half and seeded
1/2 lb	(250 g) crab (or crab substitute)
12	cherry tomatoes
1	cucumber, cut in two, seeded and sliced
1	orange cut into wedges
1	lemon cut into wedges
1 1/2 cups	(375 ml) finely chopped spinach
2 tbsp	(25 ml) mayonnaise
1/2 tsp	(2 ml) hot sauce
	salt and pepper, to taste
8	spinach leaves

GARNISH

8	sprigs of mint leaves

Use a melon baller to cut decorative balls from the melons. The honeydew rind can be used to hold the salad by cutting it into the shape of large triangles. In a bowl, combine the melon balls, spinach, crab, tomatoes, cucumber, orange and lemon wedges, mayonnaise and hot sauce; season to taste.

Line 4 plates with spinach leaves. Place the honeydew rinds on top of the spinach and fill them with the salad. Decorate with mint leaves and serve.

CANTALOUPE STUFFED WITH BERRIES AND CHICKEN

4 SERVINGS
Preparation Time: 25 minutes
Cooking Time: none

1	cantaloupe, cut in half and seeded
1 1/2 cups	(375 ml) cooked chicken, cut in cubes
2 tbsp	(25 ml) finely chopped chives
1/3 cup	(75 ml) chopped celery
1/3 cup	(75 ml) plain yogurt
3 tbsp	(50 ml) raspberries, fresh or frozen, puréed
2 tsp	(10 ml) raspberry vinegar

GARNISH

pink peppercorns
raspberries

With a melon baller, scoop out the cantaloupe or simply remove the fruit and dice. Keep the halves of the cantaloupe, taking care to leave a little bit of fruit on the rind.

Mix together the cantaloupe, chicken, celery and chives. Set aside. Mix the yogurt with the raspberry purée and raspberry vinegar.

Add half of the raspberry dressing to the mixture of cantaloupe and chicken, toss delicately.

Fill each half of cantaloupe with the mixture and cover with the remainder of the dressing. Garnish with pink peppercorns and raspberries.

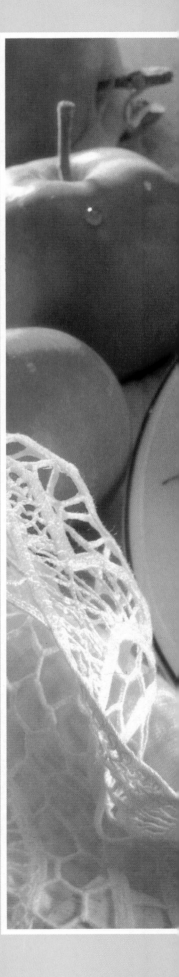

ASPARAGUS STUFFED CRÊPES

4 SERVINGS

Preparation Time: 15 minutes
Cooking Time: 25 minutes

CRÊPE BATTER
1	egg
1 cup	(250 ml) milk
3/4 cup	(175 ml) all-purpose flour
1	pinch of salt
1 tsp	(5 ml) vegetable oil

SAUCE
1 tsp	(5 ml) vegetable oil
1	green onion, finely chopped
1/4 cup	(50 ml) finely chopped celery
1/2 cup	(125 ml) dry white wine or chicken stock, skimmed of fat
1 cup	(250 ml) chicken stock, skimmed of fat
1 tbsp	(15 ml) cornstarch, diluted in a little water
	salt and pepper, to taste
1/2 cup	(125 ml) plain yogurt
1/2 cup	(125 ml) chopped, fresh basil

FILLING
1 1/2 cups	(375 ml) of vegetables (carrots, leeks and celery), julienned
1	green onion, finely chopped
2 tbsp	(25 ml) chopped, fresh parsley
10 oz	(284 ml) asparagus tips, cut in half
	salt and pepper, to taste

CRÊPES

In a food processor or with an electric mixer, mix together the egg, milk, flour and salt. In a non-stick pan, heat the oil and pour in enough batter to evenly cover the bottom of the pan. Cook for a few seconds on each side until lightly browned. Repeat the process, using all of the crêpe batter and set aside.

SAUCE

In a pan, heat the oil, and sauté the green onion and celery. Add the white wine and chicken stock. Let simmer for 10 minutes over medium heat. Thicken with cornstarch and season. When ready to serve, incorporate the yogurt and fresh basil.

FILLING

Preheat the oven to 350°F (180°C). In a bowl, mix together the julienned vegetables, green onion, parsley and asparagus tips. Season and fill the crêpes with this mixture. Roll up the crêpes and place on a greased cookie sheet. Bake in the oven for 10 to 12 minutes. Arrange each plate with a crêpe and cover with basil sauce.

FRUITY CHICKEN AND BAGEL BROCHETTES

4 SERVINGS

Preparation Time: 15 minutes
Cooking Time: 10 minutes

2 tsp	(10 ml) vegetable oil
12	cubes of chicken for brochettes
	salt and pepper, to taste
8	strawberries
1	bagel, cubed
1	kiwi, cut in 4
1/2	apple, cut in 4 and dipped in lemon juice

In a frying pan, brown the chicken cubes for 8 to 10 minutes depending on the size; season and let cool.

Place a strawberry on each skewer, then a chicken cube, a bagel cube, a piece of apple, another chicken cube and finish with a strawberry.

When ready to serve, heat in the oven or microwave.

Accompany with plain yogurt.

SMOKED SALMON AND GOAT CHEESE ROLLS

4 SERVINGS

Preparation Time: 20 minutes

Cooking Time: 2 minutes

8 oz	(250 g)	goat cheese
1/4 cup	(50 ml)	butter
1/2 cup	(125 ml)	chopped, fresh basil or 1 tsp (5 ml) dry basil
1/2		red pepper, diced
1/2 lb	(250 g)	smoked salmon, sliced
1/2 tsp	(2 ml)	pepper
1/2 cup	(50 ml)	olive oil
1 tsp	(5 ml)	lemon juice
1 tbsp	(15 ml)	vinegar or white wine
		salt and pepper, to taste
4		slices of bread, cut in two
2 tbsp	(25 ml)	melted butter
1 tsp	(5 ml)	chopped, fresh parsley

GARNISH

	zest of 1 lemon
1	tomato, seeded and diced
4	sprigs of parsley

With a food processor, mix together the goat cheese, butter and basil. Add the red pepper and mix with a spoon, set aside.

On a flat surface, spread out the sliced smoked salmon. Carefully spread the cheese mixture onto each slice and roll up.

Cover with plastic wrap and refrigerate for 2 to 3 hours. In a bowl, whisk together the olive oil, lemon juice, and wine vinegar. Season and set aside.

Place the bread on a cookie sheet and brush with a mixture of melted butter and parsley. Grill under the broiler on both sides until golden.

On a cutting board, slice the smoked salmon rolls into 16 pieces and place 4 slices on each plate; dress with the vinaigrette. Garnish with lemon zest, diced tomatoes, sprigs of basil and toast.

TROUT MEDALLIONS

4 SERVINGS
Preparation Time: 15 minutes
Cooking Time: 15 minutes

3 tbsp (40 ml) butter
2 8 oz (250 g) trout fillets, skinned, deboned and cut in the shape of medallions
2 tbsp (25 ml) chopped shallots
1 cup (250 ml) dry white wine
1 cup (250 ml) fish stock or chicken stock, skimmed of fat
1 tbsp (15 ml) all-purpose flour
3 medium egg yolks
2 tomatoes, seeded and diced
2 tbsp (25 ml) chopped, fresh tarragon or 1 tsp (5 ml) dry tarragon
1/2 cup (125 ml) 35% cream, whipped
3 cups (750 ml) chopped lettuce of your choice
1 tbsp (15 ml) olive oil
GARNISH
cherry tomatoes
fresh tarragon

In a frying pan, melt 2 tbsp (25 ml) of butter and cook the trout medallions over low heat for 1 minute on each side. Add the shallots and white wine; cover and poach for 1 to 2 minutes over low heat.

Remove the trout medallions from the pan, place on a pie plate and keep warm. Add the fish stock to the frying pan, and reduce by half over medium heat. Thicken with a mixture of flour and butter.

Remove from the stove, incorporate the egg yolks and whip. Add the diced tomatoes, tarragon and whipped cream; mix lightly until the mixture is smooth.

Cover the trout medallions with the sauce and grill under the broiler for 1 to 2 minutes, until the sauce is golden.

In a frying pan, heat the olive oil and lightly sauté the lettuce. Serve the trout medallions on a bed of lettuce. Garnish with the cherry tomatoes and fresh tarragon.

RHUBARB
AND HONEY JAM

4 SERVINGS
Preparation Time: 10 minutes
Cooking Time: 25 minutes

2 cups   (500 ml) rhubarb, peeled and cut into small pieces
1/2 cup (125 ml) honey
1/4 cup (50 ml) unsweetened orange juice
            zest of 1 orange

In a saucepan, bring all of the ingredients to a boil. Cover and cook over low heat for 20 minutes. In a food processor or with an electric mixer, purée and let cool.

Serve on toast.

A NORWEGIAN SPREAD

4 SERVINGS
Preparation Time: 15 minutes
Cooking Time: none

1 cup   (250 ml) canned sardines in oil (or smoked salmon)
2   hard boiled eggs, medium sized
2 tbsp   (25 ml) mayonnaise
2 tbsp   (25 ml) lemon juice
2 tbsp   (25 ml) old fashioned grainy mustard
            salt and pepper, to taste
1/4 cup (50 ml) finely chopped celery
2 tbsp   (25 ml) capers, drained
4   slices of bread, crusts removed and toasted

Using a food processor, purée the sardines, eggs, mayonnaise, lemon juice and mustard; season.

Add the celery and capers, mix well and refrigerate.

Spread onto the toast, and cut each slice in four.

BANANA JAM

3 TO 4 JARS

Preparation Time: 10 minutes

Cooking Time: 15 minutes

1 1/3 lb	(650 g) bananas, peeled
	juice of 1 lemon
	juice of 1/2 grapefruit
1	1 in (2 cm) piece of fresh ginger, grated
1 cup	(250 ml) water
1/2	package of pectin
1 1/2 lb	(750 g) sugar
1/2	stick of butter

GARNISH

1	banana, cubed

On a plate, crush the bananas and sprinkle with lemon and grapefruit juice.

In a saucepan, mix together the bananas, ginger and water. Cover and let simmer for 10 minutes.

In a bowl, mix the pectin with 1 1/2 tbsp (22 ml) of sugar. Stir and add the bananas. Bring to a high boil for 2 minutes, while stirring.

Add the remaining sugar and butter. Boil again for 2 minutes, stirring continuously. Garnish with the cubed bananas.

EXOTIC FRUIT JAM

6 JARS

Preparation Time: 20 minutes
Cooking Time: 30 minutes

2	grapefruits, with skin, cut into thin slices
1	pineapple, cored, peeled and cut into small pieces
1 cup	(250 ml) water
6	kiwis, peeled and cut into thin strips
2	mangos, peeled and diced
	juice of 1 lime
1	package of pectin
1/2 cup	(125 ml) maple syrup
1 tbsp	(15 ml) white rum
2 tbsp	(25 ml) maple liqueur
2 tsp	(10 ml) butter

In a small saucepan, combine the grapefruit, pineapple and water; simmer for 10 minutes.

Add the kiwis, mangos and lime juice. Continue cooking over low heat for 10 minutes. Using a potato masher, mash the fruit in the cooking juice.

In a bowl, mix the pectin with 1/2 cup (50 ml) of maple syrup. Slowly stir this mixture into the fruit mixture. While stirring, bring to and maintain a strong boil for 2 minutes.

Add the remaining maple syrup, white rum, maple liqueur and butter. Boil again for another 2 minutes, while stirring continuosly. Strain if necessary. Pour into hot, sterilized jars; seal well.

TUNA AND CHEESE SPREAD

4 SERVINGS

Preparation Time: 15 minutes
Cooking Time: none

- **1** can of tuna
- **1/2 cup** (125 ml) cream cheese with chives
- **2 tbsp** (25 ml) chopped celery
- **2 tbsp** (25 ml) chopped red pepper
- **1** green onion, finely chopped
- **4** slices of bread

GARNISH

chives
diced tomato

In a food processor, mix together the tuna, cream cheese, celery, red pepper and green onion. Spread the tuna mixture on the slices of bread. Garnish with chives and diced tomatoes.

POTATOES AU GRATIN

4 SERVINGS

Preparation Time: 15 minutes
Cooking Time: 30 minutes

- **4** medium potatoes, peeled
- **1 cup** (250 ml) chicken stock
- **1 cup** (250 ml) beer
- **1** slice of ham, diced
- **1** tomato, seeded and diced
- **1 tbsp** (15 ml) chopped, fresh parsley
- **1/2 cup** (125 ml) grated white cheddar cheese

In a pot, bring the chicken stock and beer to a boil; let reduce by one half.

Preheat the oven to 350°F (180°C). On a cutting board, cut the potatoes into thin slices; place them in 4 greased molds or muffin molds, cover with chicken stock and bake in the oven for 20 minutes or until the potatoes are almost cooked.

Remove from the oven, layer with ham, parsley, tomatoes and cheese, and continue baking for 10 to 15 minutes until brown. Serve as a side dish.

DOWN HOME BULGUR

4 SERVINGS

Preparation Time: 15 minutes
Cooking Time: 10 minutes

1 cup	(250 ml) bulgur
1 cup	(250 ml) water
1 tsp	(5 ml) vegetable oil
1 cup	(250 ml) cooked potatoes, diced
8	slices of bacon, cooked and finely chopped
2	sausages, of your choice, cooked and finely chopped
1	green onion, finely chopped
1 tbsp	(15 ml) chopped, fresh parsley salt and pepper, to taste

In a bowl, let the bulgur soak in room temperature water for 30 minutes and set aside.

In a frying pan, heat the oil, and sauté the potatoes for 5 minutes over medium heat. Add the bacon, sausages, green onions, parsley and bulgur. Season to taste and serve.

COUNTRY TIME POTATOES

4 SERVINGS

Preparation Time: 10 minutes
Cooking Time: 20 minutes

2 tsp	(10 ml) butter
1 1/2 cups	(375 ml) cooked potatoes, cubed
1/2 cup	(50 ml) cooked lean ham, diced
1/2	green or red pepper, diced
1	green onion, finely chopped salt and pepper, to taste
1 tbsp	(15 ml) chopped, fresh parsley

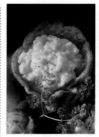

In a non-stick frying pan, melt the butter and sauté the potatoes over medium heat for 5 minutes. Incorporate the ham, peppers, and green onion; season. Cook for 5 minutes. Add the parsley and serve.

TUNA AND EGG ROLLS

4 SERVINGS

Preparation Time: 15 minutes
Cooking Time: 12 minutes

6 1/2 oz	(184 g) flaked tuna
4	hard boiled eggs
1	green onion, finely chopped
8	green olives, coarsely chopped
1 tbsp	(15 ml) chopped, fresh parsley
	salt and pepper, to taste
8	slices of bread
1 tbsp	(15 ml) melted butter
1 1/2 cups	(375 ml) cream of celery soup, hot

Preheat the oven to 400°F (200°C). In a bowl, mix together the tuna, eggs, green onion, olives and parsley; season and set aside.

On a flat surface, flatten the slices of bread with the help of a rolling pin. Spread the tuna and egg mixture on the bread.

Roll up and hold together with toothpicks if necessary. Brush lightly with melted butter and place on a greased cookie sheet. Bake for 10 to 12 minutes. Pour the cream of celery soup over top.

STUFFED TOMATOES

4 SERVINGS

Preparation Time: 10 minutes
Cooking Time: 10 minutes

1 tbsp	(15 ml) melted butter
2	slices of bread, diced
1 tbsp	(15 ml) chopped, fresh parsley
2 tbsp	(25 ml) chopped pistachios
1/2 tsp	(2 ml) minced garlic
	salt and pepper, to taste
2	tomatoes, seeded and cut in half

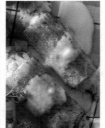

Preheat the oven to 375°F (190°C). In a bowl, mix together the butter, bread, parsley, pistachios and garlic; season. Fill each tomato with this mixture. Place on a greased cookie sheet and bake for 10 minutes.

ITALIAN BREAD

2 LOAVES
Preparation Time: 1 hour
Cooking Time: 25 minutes

1 3/4 cups	(425 ml)	hot water
2		packages of yeast
2 tsp	(10 ml)	salt
5 cups	(1.25 L)	all-purpose flour

Pour a 1/2 cup (125 ml) of hot water in a large bowl. Sprinkle the yeast in the water, let set for 10 minutes and then stir. Add the remaining water, salt and 2 cups (500 ml) of flour. Stir well. Add sufficient flour (2 cups, 500 ml) to form a firm dough.

On a floured surface, knead the dough until it is smooth and supple (6 to 8 minutes). Form into a ball and place in a well-buttered bowl. Cover with plastic wrap. Let rise in a warm place until doubled in volume (approximately 30 minutes).

Knead the dough, and divide it in two. On a floured surface, roll out the dough into a circle about 12 in (30 cm) in diameter. Tightly roll up the dough to form a cylinder (like a jellyroll).

Pinch the seams closed. Place in a buttered pan, cover with plastic wrap and let rise for 30 minutes (the dough will double in volume).

Preheat the oven to 400°F (200°C). Sprinkle a little of the flour on the dough and make 3 or 4 shallow cuts on the surface. Bake for 25 minutes.

CHICKEN LIVER PÂTÉ WITH PISTACHIOS

4 TO 6 SERVINGS
Preparation Time: 20 minutes
Cooking Time: 10 minutes

1/2 lb	(250 g) chicken livers
2 cups	(500 ml) water
1/4 cup	(50 ml) butter
1	onion, chopped
1	garlic clove, minced
2 tbsp	(25 ml) cognac or brandy
2 tbsp	(25 ml) 35% cream
1/2 cup	(125 ml) coarsely chopped pistachios

Rinse and dry the chicken livers. In a pot, bring the water to a boil and poach the chicken livers for 5 minutes. Drain and set aside.

In a non-stick frying pan, melt the butter over medium heat; sauté the onion and garlic.

Add the chicken livers and cook for approximately 4 minutes. Let cool for 5 to 6 minutes.

In a food processor, reduce the liver and onion to a purée. Add the cognac and incorporate the cream.

At medium speed, add the pistachios and mix quickly until you obtain a smooth texture without crushing the pistachios entirely.

Pour into one or more molds. Cover and refrigerate. Serve on canapés or as an appetizer.

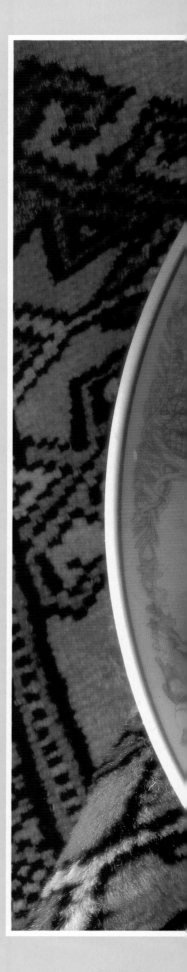

EGGS AU GRATIN
WITH BROCCOLI COULIS

4 SERVINGS

Preparation Time: 10 minutes

Cooking Time: 15 minutes

1 cup	(250 ml)	chicken stock, skimmed of fat
1 tbsp	(15 ml)	butter
1 tbsp	(15 ml)	all-purpose flour
1 1/3 cups	(325 ml)	15% cream
1 cup	(250 ml)	cooked broccoli
		salt and pepper, to taste
1 tsp	(5 ml)	butter
4		medium eggs
4		slices of bread, toasted
4		slices of cheddar cheese

In a pot, heat the chicken stock. Mix together the butter and flour and add to the chicken stock. Let simmer for 5 minutes over low heat.

Stir in the cream and remove from heat.

With a food processor or an electric mixer, mix together the sauce and the broccoli; season. Return the pot to the stove over low heat (do not boil). If the sauce is too thick, add a little cream or milk.

In a frying pan, melt the butter and cook the eggs sunny side up. Place the eggs on the toast; cover with a cheese slice, place on a cookie sheet and brown under the broiler for 1 to 2 minutes.

Serve warm with the broccoli coulis.

EGGS AU GRATIN "POMODORO"

4 SERVINGS

Preparation Time: 10 minutes

Cooking Time: 20 minutes

2 tsp	(10 ml) olive oil
2 tbsp	(25 ml) chopped shallots
1/2 cup	(175 ml) diced tomatoes
	salt and pepper, to taste
1 tsp	(5 ml) cornstarch, diluted in a little water
4 cups	(1 L) water
2 tbsp	(25 ml) white vinegar
4	eggs
4	slices of English muffin, toasted
4	slices of cooked ham
1/2 cup	(125 ml) tomato sauce
1 cup	(250 ml) grated, white cheddar cheese

In a pan, heat the olive oil and sauté the shallots. Add the tomatoes and let simmer over low heat for 10 to 15 minutes. Season and thicken with cornstarch; keep warm.

In a pot, bring the water to a boil. Lower the heat, bringing the water to a simmer. Add the vinegar, then break the eggs into the pot, one at a time. Poach for 1 to 2 minutes to your desired taste, drain and set aside.

Place the English muffins on a cookie sheet, layer with the cooked ham, poached eggs, tomato sauce and cheese. Place in the oven under the broiler and brown.

WESTERN STYLE POACHED EGGS

4 SERVINGS
Preparation Time: 20 minutes
Cooking Time: 5 minutes

4 cups	(1 L) water
2 tbsp	(25 ml) white vinegar
4	eggs
1 tsp	(5 ml) olive oil
1	green onion, finely chopped
1/4 cup	(50 ml) chopped celery
1/2 cup	(125 ml) diced green or red pepper, diced
6 oz	(180 g) ham, cooked and diced
1	tomato, seeded and diced
1 tbsp	(15 ml) chopped, fresh parsley
4	slices of bread, lightly toasted

GARNISH
lettuce
raw vegetables, of choice

In a pot, bring the water to a boil; lower the heat until the water simmers. Add the vinegar and break the eggs delicately, one at a time, into the water. Poach for 1 to 2 minutes as desired.

In a pan, heat the oil and sauté the green onion, celery, green or red pepper, ham, tomato and parsley; keep warm.

Garnish each slice of bread with the ham mixture, cover with a poached egg and place in the center of the plates. Accompany with lettuce and raw vegetables.

EGG, TOMATO AND MUSHROOM CASSEROLE

4 SERVINGS
Preparation Time: 10 minutes
Cooking Time: 30 minutes

1/4 cup	(50 ml) olive oil
2	green onions, finely chopped
2 cups	(500 ml) finely chopped mushrooms
1 tsp	(5 ml) minced garlic
19 oz	(540 ml) peeled tomatoes with fine herbs, cut into chunks
341 ml	(12 oz) beer
8	medium eggs
	salt and pepper, to taste
8	slices of bacon, cooked and crumbled
1 cup	(250 ml) white cheddar cheese, grated
2 tbsp	(25 ml) chopped, fresh parsley

Preheat the oven to 350°F (180°C). In a large ovenproof casserole, heat the oil and cook the green onions and mushrooms.

Add the garlic, tomatoes and beer; let simmer for 10 to 15 minutes.

Break the eggs into the tomatoes, and space throughout the pan; season.

Sprinkle with the bacon and the cheese and bake for 10 minutes or to your desired taste. When serving, garnish with fresh parsley.

EGGS AU GRATIN WITH HAM

4 SERVINGS
Preparation Time: 10 minutes
Cooking Time: 10 minutes

1 tsp (5 ml) butter
  4 eggs
    salt and pepper, to taste
  4 slices of bread, toasted
  4 slices of cooked ham, hot
  1 package of spinach, cooked
    and warm
    cheddar cheese, to taste

In a large frying pan, melt the butter and cook the eggs for 1 to 2 minutes on each side, to desired taste; season.

Layer each slice of toast with spinach, ham, an egg and cheese.

Place on a cookie sheet and brown in the oven for 2 to 3 minutes under the broiler. Accompany with a green salad.

POACHED EGGS NEAPOLITAN

4 SERVINGS
Preparation Time: 10 minutes
Cooking Time: 22 minutes

TOMATO SAUCE
  2 tsp (10 ml) vegetable oil
1/4 cup (50 ml) chopped onions
  1 tsp (5 ml) minced garlic
 19 oz (540 ml) crushed tomatoes
    with fine herbs
  2 tsp (10 ml) cornstarch, diluted in
    a little water
    salt and pepper, to taste

POACHED EGGS
 4 cups (1 L) water
 2 tbsp (25 ml) white vinegar
  4 medium eggs
  4 slices of bread, toasted and
    cut into rounds

TOMATO SAUCE

In a frying pan, heat the oil and sauté the onions. Add the garlic and tomatoes; let simmer over low heat for 15 to 20 minutes. Thicken the sauce with the cornstarch, season and keep warm.

POACHED EGGS

In a saucepan, bring the water to a boil and then lower the heat so the water simmers. Add the white vinegar and break the eggs, one by one, into the water. Poach for 1 to 2 minutes, to your desired taste.

Drain the eggs and place them on the toast. Cover with tomato sauce and serve.

OMELET WITH TOMATO SAUCE

4 SERVINGS
Preparation Time: 15 minutes
Cooking Time: 20 minutes

TOMATO SAUCE
2 tsp	(10 ml) vegetable oil
2	green onions, finely chopped
1	small green pepper sliced into thin strips
1	small red pepper sliced into thin strips
1/2 tsp	(2 ml) minced garlic
19 oz	(540 ml) crushed tomatoes, with fine herbs
	chili pepper flakes, to taste
	salt and pepper, to taste
1 tsp	(5 ml) cornstarch, diluted in a little water

OMELET
8	medium eggs
1/2 cup	(125 ml) milk
1/2 tsp	(2 ml) dry oregano
1/4 tsp	(1 ml) ground cumin
2 tbsp	(25 ml) chopped, fresh coriander or 1/2 tsp (2 ml) ground coriander
	salt and pepper, to taste
1 tbsp	(15 ml) butter

GARNISH
4	sprigs of fresh coriander or parsley

TOMATO SAUCE

In a saucepan, heat the oil and lightly sauté the onions and peppers. Add the garlic, tomatoes and the chili peppers. Season and let simmer over low heat for 15 to 20 minutes. Thicken with cornstarch and keep warm.

OMELETS

Divide all of the ingredients into two bowls, except for the butter. Using one or two non-stick frying pans, melt the butter and pour in the egg mixture. Cook the omelets. When serving, pour the tomato sauce over the omelets and garnish with the coriander.

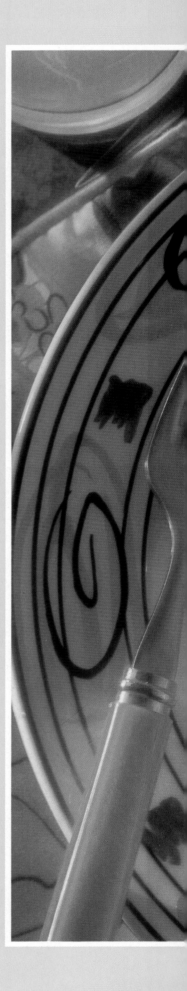

TEX-MEX SCRAMBLED EGGS

4 SERVINGS
Preparation Time: 10 minutes
Cooking Time: 10 minutes

2 tsp (10 ml) vegetable oil
6 oz (180 g) beef, cut into strips
1 green onion, chopped
1/2 red pepper, finely chopped
8 medium eggs
2 tbsp (25 ml) milk
1/2 tsp (2 ml) dried oregano
ground cumin, to taste
salt and pepper, to taste

GARNISH
4 cherry tomatoes
8 miniature corns
4 sprigs of fresh parsley

In a frying pan, heat the oil and sauté the beef, green onion, and red pepper. Add the eggs, milk, oregano and cumin; season to taste.

Garnish with cherry tomatoes, miniature corns and parsley. Serve.

BELLEVUE POACHED EGGS

4 SERVINGS
Preparation Time: 10 minutes
Cooking Time: 5 minutes

4 cups (1 L) water
2 tbsp (25 ml) white vinegar
4 medium eggs
4 slices of bread, toasted
1/2 package of spinach, blanched
and warm
4 slices of tomatoes
4 slices of cheddar cheese

In a saucepan, bring the water to a boil and then lower the heat so that the water simmers. Add the vinegar and break the eggs, one by one, into the water. Poach for 1 to 2 minutes, or to your desired taste.

Drain and place on the slices of toast. Garnish with spinach and slices of tomatoes. Cover with a slice of cheese, place on a cookie sheet and grill under the broiler for 1 minute or until the cheese has melted.

POACHED EGGS CARBONARA

4 SERVINGS

Preparation Time: 15 minutes
Cooking Time: 15 minutes

4	slices of bread
2 tbsp	(25 ml) melted butter

SAUCE

1 tsp	(5 ml) vegetable oil
1	green onion, finely chopped
1 tbsp	(15 ml) all-purpose flour
1 cup	(250 ml) milk
1/2 cup	(125 ml) 15% cream
1/4 cup	(50 ml) Parmesan cheese, grated
8	slices of bacon, cooked and chopped

POACHED EGGS

4 cups	(1 L) water
2 tbsp	(25 ml) white vinegar
4	medium eggs

Preheat the oven to 375°F (190°C). Butter the bread on both sides, and place them in four ovenproof ramekins. Flatten the bread so they fit the contours of the ramekins. Toast in the oven until golden, approximately 4 to 5 minutes. Remove from the mold and set aside.

SAUCE

In a saucepan, heat the oil and brown the onion. Sprinkle with flour; incorporate the milk, cream and cheese. Let simmer over low heat for 5 minutes and add the bacon. Keep warm.

POACHED EGGS

In a pan, bring the water to a boil, and then lower the heat until the water simmers. Add the vinegar and break the eggs, one by one, into the water. Poach for 1 to 2 minutes, to desired taste.

Drain and place each egg on a piece of toast and cover with the sauce.

POACHED EGGS WITH SMOKED SALMON

4 SERVINGS

Preparation Time: 10 minutes
Cooking Time: 15 minutes

CREAM SAUCE

2 tbsp	(25 ml) butter
2 tbsp	(25 ml) all-purpose flour
1 1/2 cups	(375 ml) hot milk
1/2 cup	(125 ml) 35% cream
	salt and pepper, to taste

POACHED EGGS

4 cups	(1 L) water
2 tbsp	(25 ml) white vinegar
4	medium eggs
4	slices of round bread, toasted
6 oz	(180 g) sliced smoked salmon
1/2	package of spinach, washed, drained and blanched
1 cup	(250 ml) grated cheddar cheese

CREAM SAUCE

In a saucepan, melt the butter and add the flour; mix well. Add the milk and cream, let simmer over low heat for 5 minutes; season and keep warm.

POACHED EGGS

In a saucepan, bring the water to a boil, and then lower the heat until the water simmers. Add the vinegar and then break the eggs, one by one. Poach for 1 to 2 minutes to your desired taste. Remove from the water and set aside.

Place the toast on a cookie sheet and place the smoked salmon on top, and form a nest on each toast. Place the spinach in the center, layer with a poached egg, cover with sauce and sprinkle with cheese. Brown for 1 to 2 minutes under the broiler.

EGGS BENEDICT WITH CHICKEN SAUSAGES

4 SERVINGS

Preparation Time: 40 minutes
Cooking Time: 10 minutes

4	English muffins, cut in half and toasted
4	medium eggs, poached

CHICKEN SAUSAGES

1 lb	(500 g) ground chicken
1 1/2 tsp	(7 ml) ground sage
1/2 tsp	(2 ml) garlic powder
1/2 tsp	(2 ml) onion powder
1/2 tsp	(2 ml) ground nutmeg
1	dash of ground cinnamon
1	dash of ground clove
	salt and pepper, to taste

HOLLANDAISE SAUCE

2	medium egg yolks
2 tbsp	(25 ml) Dijon mustard
2 tbsp	(25 ml) lemon juice
1	pinch of salt
1	pinch of Cayenne pepper
1/2 cup	(50 ml) melted butter
2 tbsp	(25 ml) olive oil
2	medium egg whites
1	pinch of cream of tartar

CHICKEN SAUSAGES

In a food processor, mix together all of the ingredients. Divide the mixture into eight parts and form patties of 3 to 4 in (6 to 8 cm) in diameter. In a non-stick pan, cook the chicken sausages for 3 minutes on each side. Remove from the pan, place on paper towel and keep warm.

HOLLANDAISE SAUCE

With a food processor or a mixer, mix together the egg yolks, Dijon mustard, lemon juice, salt and Cayenne pepper. Gradually add the melted butter and the olive oil.

In a bowl whip the egg whites with the cream of tartar, and then slowly incorporate the Hollandaise sauce.

Place the toasted English muffins on the plates and layer with the chicken sausage, and poached egg. Cover with the Hollandaise sauce. If you wish, you can put them under the broiler to achieve a golden color. Serve immediately.

ENGLISH MUFFINS WITH SAUSAGE AND SPINACH

4 SERVINGS

Preparation Time: 15 minutes
Cooking Time: 10 minutes

SAUCE

- **1 cup** (250 ml) sour cream
- **1 tbsp** (25 ml) Dijon mustard
- **1 tbsp** (15 ml) chopped, fresh parsley
  salt and pepper, to taste
- **4** English muffins, cut in half and toasted
- **4 to 5** sausages, cut in half and grilled
- **1** package of spinach, washed, blanched and warm

In a bowl, mix together the sour cream, mustard and parsley; season and set aside. Garnish each muffin with spinach and sausage. Cover with sauce and serve.

GOOD MORNING CLUB SANDWICH

4 SERVINGS

Preparation Time: 10 minutes
Cooking Time: 5 minutes

- **1 tsp** (5 ml) butter
- **2** medium eggs
  salt and pepper, to taste
- **2** slices of cheddar cheese
- **6** pieces of toast
- **8** spinach leaves, washed and dried
- **2** slices of ham
- **8** slices of tomatoes
- **2** lettuce leaves, of choice

In a frying pan, melt the butter and fry the eggs on both sides; season. Place an egg, a slice of cheese, and a spinach leaf on a piece of toast. Cover with another piece of toast. Place a slice of ham, tomato and lettuce leaf on the toast and cover with another piece of toast.

Insert 4 toothpicks in each corner and cut diagonally, twice. Serve.

GRILLED CHEESE BAGEL

4 SERVINGS

Preparation Time: 10 minutes

Cooking Time: 5 minutes

2	bagels
6 oz	(180 g) cheese slices, of choice
4 cups	(1 L) lettuce, of choice
1	apple cut into thin slices
1/4 cup	(50 ml) walnuts

On a cutting board, slice the bagels in two horizontally; place them on a cookie sheet, layer with cheese and grill in the oven under the broiler.

Place the bagels on a bed of lettuce; garnish with slices of apples and walnuts.

Dress the lettuce with your favorite vinaigrette.

ENGLISH MUFFINS WITH SMOKED SALMON

4 SERVINGS

Preparation Time: 15 minutes

Cooking Time: none

1 tbsp	(15 ml) Dijon mustard
1/4 cup	(50 ml) olive oil
1 tbsp	(15 ml) wine vinegar
	salt and pepper, to taste
	lettuce of choice
1/2 cup	(125 ml) sour cream
2 tbsp	(25 ml) chopped chives
4	English muffins, toasted
1/2 cup	(125 ml) cream cheese, softened
8	slices of smoked salmon

In a bowl, mix together the mustard, olive oil and wine vinegar; season to taste. Incorporate the sour cream, and chives; mix and set aside.

Spread cream cheese on the English muffins, garnish generously with lettuce, layer with the smoked salmon and cover with chive sauce.

CORN BREAD SANDWICHES

4 SERVINGS

Preparation Time: 25 minutes
Cooking Time: 25 minutes

CORN BREAD

3/4 cup	(175 ml)	all-purpose flour
1 cup	(250 ml)	corn flour
1 tbsp	(15 ml)	sugar
2 tsp	(10 ml)	baking powder
1/2 tsp	(2 ml)	salt
1 cup	(250 ml)	milk
1		egg, beaten
1 tbsp	(15 ml)	melted butter
2 tsp	(10 ml)	cumin seeds

GARNISH

1/4 cup	(50 ml)	Dijonnaise mustard
1/2 lb	(250 g)	prosciutto, thinly sliced
1/2 lb	(250 g)	cheese of choice, sliced
1 cup	(250 g)	alfalfa sprouts
2		endive leaves

CORN BREAD

In a bowl, mix together the flour, sugar, baking powder and salt.

Add the milk, egg, melted butter and cumin seeds; mix well. Don't mix the dough too much because it will become elastic and firm, which will make a heavier bread.

Spread the dough in a lightly greased 8 in (20 cm) loaf pan.

Bake at 425°F (220°C) for 20 to 25 minutes or until the top is golden. Remove from the pan, let cool on a wire rack.

Slice the corn bread in two, horizontally, and then in four. Spread Dijonnaise mustard on each bottom slice and garnish with prosciutto and cheese.

Garnish with alfalfa sprouts and endive leaves. Cover with the remaining slices of bread and serve.

CHICKEN SANDWICH WITH ROASTED ALMONDS

4 SERVINGS

Preparation Time: 15 minutes

Cooking Time: none

8	slices of whole wheat bread
1 1/2 cups	(375 ml) cooked chicken, chopped
1/2	stalk of celery, chopped
2 tbsp	(25 ml) chopped red onion
1/2 cup	(125 ml) mayonnaise
1 tbsp	(15 ml) Dijon mustard
1/4 cup	(50 ml) thinly sliced, roasted almonds
2 tbsp	(25 ml) chopped chives
	salt and pepper, to taste

Toast the bread. In a bowl, mix together all the remaining ingredients. Adjust the seasonings to taste. Spread the mixture onto 4 pieces of toast and cover with the remaining toast.

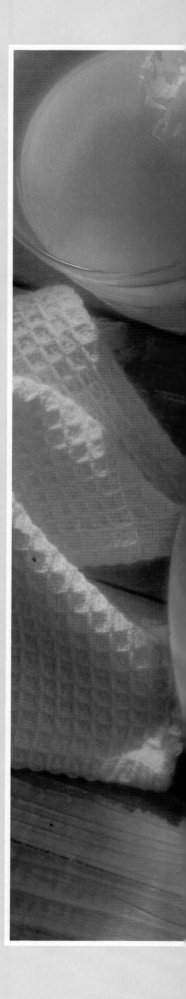

KAISER ROLLS WITH TUNA STUFFING

4 SERVINGS

Preparation Time: 15 minutes
Cooking Time: none

2 tbsp	(25 ml) corn oil
2 tbsp	(25 ml) lemon juice
2	garlic cloves, minced
4	Kaiser rolls
4	lettuce leaves
4	anchovy fillets (optional)
12	black olives, pitted

STUFFING

1/2 cup	(125 ml) cucumber, cut in half rings
2	tomatoes, cut in quarters
1/2 cup	(125 ml) finely chopped green peppers
2	green onions, cut in rings
13 oz	(368 g) tuna in water, drained
2 tbsp	(25 ml) chopped, fresh parsley salt and pepper, to taste

In a small bowl, mix together the oil, lemon juice and garlic.

Cut the kaiser rolls in half and set aside the top half. Remove the soft inner bread from the lower portion and lightly brush the interior with the oil mixture; set aside.

Gently mix together the ingredients for the stuffing.

Place a lettuce leaf on the bottom of each roll and stuff with the tuna stuffing.

Garnish each roll with anchovies and black olives and cover with the top part of the roll. Serve.

CHICKEN AND HAM CROISSANTS

4 SERVINGS

Preparation time: 15 minutes
Cooking Time: 5 minutes

4	croissants
2	chicken breasts, skinless, boneless, cooked and thinly sliced
4 1/2 oz	(125 g) cooked ham, thinly sliced
12	spinach leaves, blanched
1 cup	(250 ml) bechamel sauce, store bought
1 cup	(250 ml) grated emmental cheese

Cut the croissants lengthwise.

Layer the lower half of the croissants with chicken, ham and spinach leaves. Keep the top part of the croissants warm.

Preheat the oven on "broil". Place the lower half of the croissants on a cookie sheet. Cover with bechamel sauce and garnish with cheese.

Broil the croissants and cover with the top half.

Serve with a green salad.

SURPRISE BREAD

8 SERVINGS
Preparation Time: 20 minutes
Cooking Time: 15 to 20 minutes

8	small sesame seed buns
1	onion, cut in cubes
1 tbsp	(15 ml) corn oil
1 lb	(500 g) lean ground beef
1 tbsp	(15 ml) beef stock, skimmed of fat
1 tbsp	(15 ml) chopped, fresh parsley
1/2 cup	(125 ml) finely grated carrots
1/2 cup	(125 ml) chopped hazelnuts
1	tomato, blanched and cut into cubes
1 cup	(250 ml) grated emmental cheese
1/2 tsp	(2 ml) pepper
1	medium egg, beaten
1 tbsp	(15 ml) melted butter

Preheat the oven to 400°F (200°C). Cut the buns in half, lengthwise (follow the seam). Scoop out the interior of each bun, leaving the outside crust intact. Keep 1 cup (250 ml) of bread for the stuffing.

In a frying pan, heat the oil, sauté the onion, add the lean ground beef and cook.

Transfer to a bowl and let cool slightly.

Combine all of the other ingredients in the bowl, except the butter. Mix well, fill each bread crust shell with the mixture.

Lightly brush the tops of the buns with the melted butter. Wrap well in aluminum foil and place on a cookie sheet. Bake for 15 to 20 minutes.

Serve with sauce of choice.

HAM AND ASPARAGUS CRÊPES

4 SERVINGS

Preparation Time: 15 minutes
Cooking Time: 20 minutes

CRÊPE BATTER

1	egg
1 cup	(250 ml) milk
3/4 cup	(175 ml) all-purpose flour
1	pinch of salt

GARNISH

2	slices of ham, cut into strips
2	potatoes, cooked and diced
1	green onion, chopped
1	stalk of celery, cut into sticks and blanched
2 tbsp	(25 ml) chopped, fresh parsley
1	can of asparagus

SAUCE

1 tbsp	(15 ml) butter
2 tbsp	(25 ml) all-purpose flour
1 cup	(250 ml) warm milk
19 oz	(540 ml) diced tomatoes
1 tbsp	(15 ml) cornstarch
1/2 cup	(125 ml) grated cheese, of choice

Preheat the oven to 400°F (200°C).

CRÊPES

Using a bowl or a food processor, mix together the egg, milk, flour and salt. In a frying pan, sprayed with a non-stick spray, pour in the batter so that it evenly covers the bottom of the pan. Cook for a few seconds on each side. Repeat this process and use all of the crêpe batter. Set the crêpes aside.

GARNISH

In another bowl, mix together the ham, potatoes, onion, celery and parsley. Stuff the crêpes with the asparagus and ham mixture. Roll the crêpes and place them on a platter. Set aside.

SAUCE

In a saucepan, melt the butter, add the flour and heat for a few seconds over low heat. Add the warm milk and let simmer for a few minutes. Add the cornstarch diluted in a little milk, and bring to a boil. Cover the crêpes with sauce and garnish with grated cheese. Brown in the oven for a few minutes.

SUNDAY MEAT LOAF

6 SERVINGS

Preparation Time: 15 minutes
Cooking Time: 1 hour

1	large zucchini
2 tbsp	(25 ml) vegetable oil
	salt and pepper, to taste
4	slices of bread
1 cup	(250 ml) milk
1	package of spinach, washed and lightly cooked
19 oz	(540 ml) crushed tomatoes with fine herbs
1 1/2 cups	(375 ml) grated white cheddar cheese

STUFFING

1 1/2 lb	(750 g) lean ground beef or turkey
2	green onions, chopped
1 tsp	(5 ml) minced garlic
2	eggs, beaten
2 tbsp	(25 ml) chopped, fresh parsley
	salt and pepper, to taste

STUFFING

Preheat the oven to 350°F (180°C). Mix together the ground beef or turkey, onions, garlic, eggs and parsley; season and set aside.

Cut the zucchini into thin slices. In a frying pan, heat the oil and cook the zucchini slices; season.

Line the bottom of a loaf pan with slices of zucchini and then 1/3 of the stuffing. Moisten two slices of bread with the milk and place over the stuffing. Add the spinach and layer with another 1/3 of the stuffing. Add two more slices of bread, moistened with milk, then the rest of the stuffing and crushed tomatoes.

Bake for 30 minutes and then sprinkle with cheese. Continue baking for another 30 minutes.

HAM AND ARTICHOKE PIE

4 TO 8 SERVINGS

Preparation Time: 40 minutes
Cooking Time: 43 minutes

2 tbsp	(25 ml) butter
2 tbsp	(25 ml) all-purpose flour
1/2 cup	(125 ml) chicken stock, skimmed of fat
1/2 cup	(125 ml) milk
2 tbsp	(25 ml) chopped, fresh parsley
1/2	lemon juice
1 tbsp	(15 ml) Dijonnaise mustard
1 cup	(250 ml) diced, cooked ham
14 oz	(398 ml) sliced artichokes
1/2 lb	(350 g) pie dough
6	medium eggs, hard boiled and sliced
1 cup	(250 ml) grated gruyère cheese
1	medium egg, beaten

In a frying pan, melt the butter and stir in the flour. Cook for 1 to 2 minutes; add the chicken stock and the milk, while mixing with a whisk. Cover and let simmer over low heat for 5 minutes.

Remove from the stove and add the parsley, lemon juice and mustard. Then add the ham and artichokes. Let cool.

Preheat the oven to 400°F (200°C). Divide the dough in two; roll out the dough with a rolling pin and place in a 10 in (25 cm) pie pan. Fill with 1/3 of the mixture, layer with the hard boiled eggs, sprinkle with cheese and cover with the remaining mixture.

Brush the sides of the dough with a beaten egg. Cover with the other pie crust and trim the sides. Brush the top with the beaten egg and pierce a hole in the center to let air escape. With any excess dough, you can decorate the top of the pie. Bake for 35 minutes. Serve.

HAM CASSEROLE WITH BARLEY

4 SERVINGS

Preparation Time: 10 minutes
Cooking Time: 35 minutes

2 tsp	(10 ml) vegetable oil
1/4 cup	(50 ml) chopped onions
1/4 cup	(50 ml) diced celery
1/4 cup	(50 ml) diced carrots
2 cups	(500 ml) chicken stock, skimmed of fat
1 cup	(250 ml) pearled barley
1 tsp	(5 ml) vegetable oil
6 oz	(180 g) ham, cooked and cut into thin strips
4	medium eggs, beaten
	salt and pepper, to taste

In a pan, heat the oil and sauté the onions, celery and carrots. Add the chicken stock and barley. Cover and simmer over medium-low heat for 30 minutes. Let cool.

In a non-stick frying pan, heat the oil and sauté the ham. Add the eggs and the barley mixture. Season and cook while stirring with a wooden spoon. Serve.

BREAKFAST PARADISIO

4 SERVINGS

Preparation Time: 10 minutes

Cooking Time: 5 minutes

- **2 tsp** (10 ml) olive oil
- **1** green onion
- **1/2** red or green pepper, diced
- **3** slices of cooked ham, diced
- **1** tomato, seeded and diced
- **1/2 tsp** (2 ml) minced garlic
- **1 tbsp** (15 ml) chopped, fresh parsley
- **1/2 tsp** (2 ml) Italian spices
- **1 cup** (250 ml) Hollandaise sauce, store bought
  salt and pepper, to taste
- **4 cups** (1 L) water
- **2 tbsp** (25 ml) vinegar
- **4** eggs
- **2** slices of round bread, (English muffin), lightly toasted
- **4** lettuce leaves

In a pan, heat the oil and sauté the green onion, red or green pepper, ham, diced tomatoes and garlic. Add the parsley, spices and Hollandaise sauce; season and keep warm.

In a saucepan, bring the water to a boil. Lower the heat until the water simmers. Add the vinegar and break the eggs, one at a time, into the water. Poach for 1 to 2 minutes to desired taste.

Drain and place each egg on a slice of bread, then place on plates. Garnish with lettuce and cover with the sauce.

CHICKEN AND EGG SALAD WITH MUSHROOMS

4 SERVINGS

Preparation Time: 10 minutes
Cooking Time: 20 minutes

4	slices of bread
2 tbsp	(25 ml) melted butter
10 oz	(284 ml) cream of mushroom soup, store bought
2	half breasts of chicken, cooked, and diced
4	medium eggs, scrambled
1 tbsp	(15 ml) chopped, fresh parsley

Preheat the oven to 375°F (190°C). Butter both sides of the bread and place in four ovenproof ramekins. Lightly brown in the oven for 4 to 5 minutes. Remove from the molds and set aside.

In a saucepan, heat the cream of mushroom soup; add the chicken and the eggs, and heat lightly.

Pour the sauce over the bread and garnish with chopped parsley.

HAM AND SWISS CHEESE BREAD

4 SERVINGS

Preparation Time: 30 minutes
Cooking Time: 1 hour

1 tsp	(5 ml) baking powder
1 cup	(250 ml) flour, sifted
3	eggs
2 tbsp	(25 ml) vegetable oil
3/4 cup	(175 ml) milk
5 oz	(150 g) grated swiss gruyère cheese
1/2 lb	(250 g) ham, cubed pepper, to taste

BECHAMEL SAUCE

1/4 cup	(50 ml) melted butter
1/2 cup	(125 ml) all-purpose flour
1 cup	(500 ml) milk
1/2	onion, pierced with cloves
1 tsp	(5 ml) salt
1	pinch of Cayenne pepper
1	pinch of nutmeg
1/4 cup	(50 ml) 15% cream
1 tsp	(5 ml) butter

Preheat the oven to 350°F (180°C). In a food processor, combine the baking powder and flour. Incorporate the eggs, oil and milk; mix.

Add the cheese and ham; mix and adjust seasoning to taste. Cover the bottom of a rectangular pan with wax paper and pour in the mixture. Let set for 10 minutes, then bake for approximately 45 minutes.

SAUCE

In a saucepan, melt the butter over low heat; add the flour and stir with a wooden spoon. Lightly cook the mixture for 2 to 3 minutes, while stirring continuously.

Gradually add the milk, stir with a whisk and add the half onion pierced with cloves. Season and let simmer for 15 to 20 minutes, while stirring frequently until the sauce becomes smooth.

Add the cream and butter, mix well. Serve the ham and Swiss cheese bread with the sauce.

SAUSAGE AU GRATIN WITH POTATOES AND BEER

4 SERVINGS
Preparation Time: 25 minutes
Cooking Time: 35 minutes

4 cups	(1 L) water
1	pinch of salt
1 cup	(250 ml) cubed carrots
1 cup	(250 ml) cubed turnips
2 cups	(500 ml) cubed potatoes
1 tsp	(5 ml) butter
1 lb	(500 g) pork and beef sausages
1/2 cup	(125 ml) chopped onion
2 tbsp	(25 ml) chopped, fresh parsley
12 oz	(341 ml) beer
2 cups	(500 ml) chicken stock, skimmed of fat
1/2 lb	(250 g) sliced provolone cheese

 In a pot, bring the water to a boil. Add the salt, carrots, turnip and potatoes; cover and simmer for 10 minutes. Drain and set aside.

In a frying pan, melt the butter and cook the sausages for 2 minutes over medium heat. Add the onions and parsley; cook for 2 more minutes.

Preheat the oven to 375°F (190°C). Place the sausages in an ovenproof dish and cover with the vegetable mixture. Add the beer and chicken stock. Garnish with the cheese slices and bake for approximately 20 minutes.

CHEESE PIE

6 TO 8 SERVINGS

Preparation Time: 40 minutes
Cooking Time: 1 hour 20 minutes

PIE CRUST
1 1/2 cups (375 ml) all-purpose flour
1 pinch of salt
1/2 cup (125 ml) butter
1/4 cup (50 ml) sour cream
1 egg yolk

CHEESE FILLING
1/4 cup (50 ml) butter
4 cups (1 L) finely chopped onion
1 cup (250 ml) 35% cream
2 medium eggs
1/2 tsp (2 ml) ground nutmeg
1 cup (250 ml) grated emmental cheese
pepper, to taste

In a food processor, mix together the flour, salt and butter. Incorporate the sour cream and egg yolk, mix until the dough holds. Form the dough into a ball, cover and refrigerate.

Preheat the oven to 400°F (200°C), roll out the dough to form a circle and place in the bottom of a 10 in (25 cm) pie pan.

In a non-stick frying pan, melt the butter and fry the onions until golden. Let cool.

Mix the cream, eggs, nutmeg and cheese in a bowl; season. Spread the onions on the dough, pour the egg mixture on top and bake for 10 minutes. Lower the heat to 325°F (160°C) and continue baking for 40 minutes. Serve hot or at room temperature.

MEXICAN CHICKEN

4 SERVINGS

Preparation Time: 10 minutes
Cooking Time: 15 minutes

1 tsp (5 ml) vegetable oil
4 half breasts of chicken, boneless, and skinless, sliced
2 tbsp (25 ml) fajita seasoning
4 slices of bread, lightly toasted
2 cups (500 ml) Mexican salsa
1 1/2 cups (375 ml) grated cheddar cheese

In a pan, heat the oil and lightly brown the chicken breasts for 1 to 2 minutes on each side, depending on their thickness. Add the fajita seasoning and finish cooking (about 5 minutes) over medium heat.

Place the slices of bread on a cookie sheet, layer with the chicken slices, Mexican salsa and cheese. Brown under the broiler for 2 to 3 minutes.

The Everyday Cooking Collection

CHOCOLATE SANDWICHES

4 SERVINGS

Preparation Time: 15 minutes
Cooking Time: 8 minutes

8	slices of bread, crust removed
1/4 cup	(50 ml) chocolate and nut spread, store bought
1 cup	(250 ml) sliced strawberries
4	eggs
1/4 cup	(50 ml) sugar
1 tsp	(5 ml) vanilla extract
1 cup	(250 ml) milk
1 tbsp	(15 ml) vegetable oil

Cover four slices of bread with the chocolate and nut spread. Place the sliced strawberries on top and cover with the other slices of bread to form a sandwich.

In a bowl, beat the eggs with the sugar, vanilla extract and milk. In a non-stick frying pan, heat 1 tbsp (15 ml) of vegetable oil over medium heat. Lightly dip a sandwich in the egg mixture and place it in the hot frying pan. Cook for 2 minutes on each side, or until golden. Serve warm.

FLAKY CHOCOLATE BREAD

4 SERVINGS

Preparation Time: 10 minutes
Cooking Time: 10 minutes

8	slices of bread
4	medium eggs
1 cup	(250 ml) milk
1/2 cup	(125 ml) icing sugar
2 tsp	(10 ml) butter
1/4 cup	(50 ml) cocoa powder
1 1/2 cups	(375 ml) mix of strawberries, raspberries and blueberries, fresh or frozen

Using a rolling pin, flatten the slices of bread and set aside.

In a bowl, mix together the eggs, milk and icing sugar. Dip the bread in the mixture, making sure to coat each side.

Melt the butter in a frying pan over medium heat, and cook the bread for 1 to 2 minutes on each side, until lightly brown.

Cut the toast in the shape of triangles. Sprinkle with the cocoa and serve with the berries.

BERRY CRÊPES WITH RASPBERRY COULIS

4 SERVINGS

Preparation Time: 20 minutes
Cooking Time: 20 minutes

CRÊPE BATTER

1	medium egg
1 cup	(250 ml) milk
3/4 cup	(175 ml) buckwheat flour
2 tsp	(10 ml) icing sugar
1	pinch of salt
1 tbsp	(15 ml) vegetable oil
2 cups	(500 ml) berries (strawberries, raspberries, blueberries, etc…) fresh or frozen
1/4 cup	(50 ml) icing sugar

RASPBERRY COULIS

2 cups	(500 ml) raspberries, fresh or frozen
1/2 cup	(125 ml) apple juice
1 tbsp	(15 ml) lemon juice
1/3 cup	(75 ml) sugar

CRÊPES

Preheat the oven to 400°F (200°C). In a bowl, mix together all the ingredients for the crêpe batter, except for the oil. In a non-stick frying pan, heat the oil and cook 4 thin crêpes over medium heat.

RASPBERRY COULIS

In a small saucepan, heat all the ingredients of the coulis and let simmer for 2 to 3 minutes. Purée in a food processor or an electric mixer, and strain. Set aside.

Garnish each crêpe with berries, cover with the raspberry coulis and fold. Place on a cookie sheet and sprinkle with icing sugar. Bake for 10 to 12 minutes and serve.

FRUIT BROCHETTES

4 SERVINGS

Preparation Time: 15 minutes
Cooking Time: 25 minutes

FRUIT BROCHETTES
- **1/2 cup** (125 ml) maple syrup
- **1 tbsp** (15 ml) butter
- **4** fresh fruit brochettes (pineapple, cantaloupe, kiwis, strawberries, apples, etc…)
- **4** sprigs of mint

CRÈME ANGLAISE
- **4** egg yolks
- **1/2 cup** (50 ml) honey
- **1 1/2 cups** (375 ml) warm milk
- **1 tsp** (5 ml) vanilla extract
- **1 tsp** (5 ml) cornstarch, diluted in a bit of milk

CRÈME ANGLAISE

In a double boiler, or in a saucepan over very low heat, mix together the egg yolks and honey. Add the warm milk, vanilla extract and cornstarch. Heat while mixing, until the cream sticks to the back of a wooden spoon. Pour into a bowl and let cool.

FRUIT BROCHETTES

In a frying pan, melt the butter and heat the fruit brochettes. Add maple syrup and let caramelize. Serve the brochettes accompanied with the Crème Anglaise and garnish with sprigs of mint.

FRENCH TOAST WITH RASPBERRY COULIS

4 SERVINGS

Preparation Time: 20 minutes
Cooking Time: 20 minutes

- **4** slices of white bread
- **4** slices of whole wheat bread
- **2 tbsp** (25 ml) butter
- **1/4 cup** (50 ml) cocoa
- **1/4 cup** (50 ml) icing sugar
- **2** apples cut into thin slices
- **2** peaches cut into thin slices
- **2** oranges cut into quarters
- **4** sprigs of fresh mint (optional)

FRENCH TOAST BATTER
- **4** medium eggs
- **2 cups** (500 ml) milk
- **1/2 cup** (125 ml) powdered sugar
- **1 tsp** (5 ml) vanilla extract

RASPBERRY COULIS
- **2 cups** (500 ml) fresh or frozen raspberries
- **1/2 cup** (125 ml) apple juice
- **1 tbsp** (15 ml) lemon juice
- **1/4 cup** (50 ml) sugar

In a bowl, mix together the ingredients of the French toast batter. Dip the eight slices of bread in the batter. In a frying pan, heat the butter and lightly brown the slices of bread. Set aside and let cool (take care not to place the slices of bread on top of one another).

RASPBERRY COULIS

In a small saucepan, heat all the ingredients of the coulis for 5 minutes. Purée the coulis using a food processor or hand mixer. Strain and set aside.

Cut the slices of bread into strips or triangles. Sprinkle the whole wheat bread with cocoa and the white bread with icing sugar.

Place the strips of bread in the center of the serving plates (alternating the wheat and white bread). Cover with the raspberry coulis; garnish with the fresh fruit, and sprigs of mint.

FRENCH TOAST WITH MAPLE CREAM

4 SERVINGS
Preparation Time: 10 minutes
Cooking Time: 5 minutes

MAPLE CREAM
1 1/2 cups (425 ml) evaporated milk
2 tbsp (25 ml) maple butter
2 tbsp (25 ml) cornstarch, diluted in water
2 medium egg yolks
1 tbsp (15 ml) butter (optional)

FRENCH TOAST
4 medium eggs
1 cup (250 ml) milk
1/2 cup (125 ml) icing sugar
1 tbsp (15 ml) butter
8 slices of bread

GARNISH
2 tbsp (25 ml) icing sugar (optional)
fresh fruit

MAPLE CREAM

In a saucepan, heat the evaporated milk and maple butter. Add the cornstarch and heat until the mixture thickens. Remove from the stove and add the 2 egg yolks and butter. Mix well and keep warm.

FRENCH TOAST

In a large bowl, using a whisk or an electric mixer, mix together the eggs, milk and icing sugar.

In a non-stick frying pan, melt the butter. Dip the slices of bread in the egg mixture and cook until golden; set aside.

Repeat with the other slices of bread.

When ready to serve, pour the maple cream on 4 serving plates. Place two slices of French toast on each plate. Garnish with fresh fruit and sprinkle with the icing sugar.

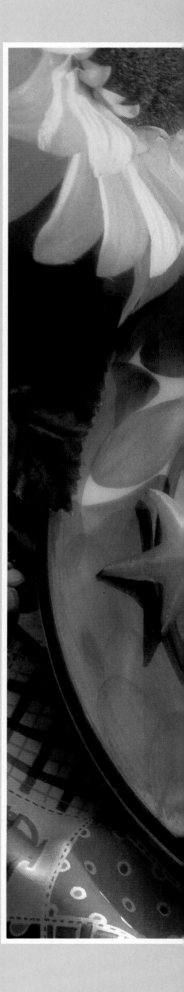

FAVORITE CRUMPETS

6 TO 8 SERVINGS
Preparation Time: 20 minutes
Cooking Time: 45 minutes

6	crumpets, cut in two
3	eggs
1 1/2 cups	(375 ml) hot maple syrup
2 tbsp	(25 ml) butter
1 tbsp	(15 ml) flour
1/2 cup	(125 ml) 15% cream
1/2 cup	(125 ml) pecans

Crumpets can be eaten anytime of the day with your favorite toppings, such as maple syrup, fruit coulis, caramel, chocolate spread, and yogurt. Here are a few delicious ideas: Preheat the oven to 350°F (180°C). Place the crumpets on a greased 9 in (23 cm) pie plate.

PECAN MAPLE CRUMPETS

Mix together the butter, flour, cream and set aside.

In a bowl, beat the eggs with an electric mixer, incorporate the hot maple syrup, butter, flour and cream.

Pour the mixture over the crumpets, garnish with pecans and bake for 35 to 40 minutes. Cool and serve.

HEALTHY CRUMPETS

Cover toasted crumpets with Ricotta cheese and fresh fruits.

MORNING CRUMPETS

Top a crumpet with a sliced boiled egg, a slice of ham and a slice of cheese, and grill in the oven.

CRUMPET SANDWICH

Fill your crumpet with mayonnaise, slices of turkey, and lettuce and cover with another crumpet. Cut in two and serve.

DELI CRUMPET

Spread cream cheese on your crumpet, add lettuce and smoked salmon. Garnish with parsley and capers.

CITRUS RICE CAKES

4 SERVINGS

Preparation Time: 15 minutes
Cooking Time: 1 hour

2	medium eggs
1/3 cup	(75 ml) brown sugar
1 1/2 cups	(375 ml) hot milk
1 tsp	(5 ml) vanilla extract
1/3 cup	(75 ml) rice
1/4 cup	(50 ml) chopped walnuts
2 tbsp	(25 ml) chopped, fresh mint (optional)
2	oranges, peeled and cut into wedges
1	grapefruit, peeled and cut into wedges

GARNISH

	fresh fruit
4	fresh mint leaves

Preheat the oven to 300°F (150°C). In a large bowl, mix together the eggs, brown sugar, milk and vanilla extract.

Add the rice, walnuts, mint, orange and grapefruit wedges.

Mix and pour into small greased ramekins or a pyrex plate and bake for approximately 1 hour.

Cool and remove from ramekins. Serve with fresh fruit and mint.

BREAD PANACHE

4 SERVINGS

Preparation Time: 15 minutes
Cooking Time: 10 minutes

1	medium egg
1 cup	(250 ml) milk
1/2 cup	(125 ml) icing sugar
4	slices of bread
1 tsp	(5 ml) butter
1 cup	(250 ml) strawberries cut in half
2	kiwis, peeled and sliced
2	peaches, quartered
2	prunes, quartered
1	apple, cut in slices
1 cup	(250 ml) frozen yogurt, vanilla

STRAWBERRY COULIS

1 cup	(250 ml) fresh or frozen strawberries
1/4 cup	(50 ml) corn syrup
1/2 cup	(125 ml) apple juice

GARNISH

	mint leaves

In a bowl, whisk the egg, milk and icing sugar. Dip the bread slices into the mixture. In a frying pan, melt the butter and cook the slices of bread for 1 minute on each side. Set aside.

In a saucepan, heat the strawberries, corn syrup and apple juice for a few minutes. Mix in a food processor, strain, and let cool.

Place the slices of bread on plates; accompany with fruits and frozen yogurt.

Cover with the strawberry coulis and garnish with mint leaves.

SNOWY STRAWBERRY CRÊPES

4 SERVINGS

Preparation Time: 15 minutes
Cooking Time: 20 minutes

1 1/2 cups	(375 ml) strawberries
4	kiwis
1	egg white
1 tbsp	(15 ml) sugar

CRÊPE BATTER

1	medium egg
3/4 cup	(175 ml) all-purpose flour
2 tsp	(10 ml) icing sugar
1 cup	(250 ml) buttermilk
1 tbsp	(15 ml) melted butter
	vanilla extract, to taste
1	pinch of salt

RASPBERRY COULIS

2 cups	(500 ml) raspberries, fresh or frozen
1/4 cup	(50 ml) water
2 tsp	(10 ml) lemon juice
1/4 cup	(50 ml) sugar

GARNISH

1/2 cup	(125 ml) ice milk
	fresh fruit

Preheat the oven to 450°F (220°C).

Clean and cut the strawberries in half. Peel the kiwis and cut them in four. In a bowl beat the egg white with the sugar to form soft peaks, and set aside.

In a bowl or food processor, mix together all the ingredients of the crêpe batter.

In a non-stick frying pan, place 3 tbsp (50 ml) of the crêpe batter and cook for 1 minute on each side over medium heat. Repeat the process until all of the batter is used. Set aside.

In a saucepan, heat the ingredients of the raspberry coulis; let simmer for 5 minutes. Strain and keep warm.

Place the strawberries and kiwis in the center of the crêpes. Cover with 2 tbsp (25 ml) of coulis and fold the crêpes in the form of a roll. Place the crêpes on a cookie sheet and brush with egg whites. Lightly brown in the oven for a few minutes.

Serve the rest of the raspberry coulis. Garnish with fresh fruits.

BREAD PUDDING

6 TO 8 SERVINGS

Preparation Time: 10 minutes
Cooking Time: 50 minutes

4	medium eggs
2 cups	(500 ml) milk
1 tsp	(5 ml) vanilla extract
1 cup	(250 ml) brown sugar
6	slices of bread cut into strips
1/2 cup	(125 ml) dried fruit
1/2 cup	(125 ml) raisins
1/2 tsp	(2 ml) ground cinnamon

Preheat the oven to 350°F (180°C). In a large bowl, beat together the eggs, milk, vanilla extract and brown sugar. Incorporate the strips of bread, dried fruit, raisins and cinnamon. Pour into a greased loaf pan and bake for 45 to 50 minutes. Cool before serving.

ORANGE FLAVORED FRENCH TOAST

4 SERVINGS
Preparation Time: 10 minutes
Cooking Time: 5 minutes

4	eggs
1 cup	(250 ml) milk
1 cup	(250 ml) icing sugar
1 tbsp	(15 ml) orange flavored flower water
2 tbsp	(25 ml) butter
8	slices of bread

GARNISH

2 tbsp	(25 ml) icing sugar
	zest of 2 oranges
	zest of 2 limes
	fresh fruit of choice

In a large bowl, with a whisk or an electric mixer, mix together the eggs, milk, icing sugar and orange flavored flower water.

In a non-stick frying pan, melt the butter. Dip a slice of bread in the egg mixture and cook until golden. Repeat the procedure for each slice of bread.

When ready to serve, garnish with the orange and lime zest and sprinkle with icing sugar. Accompany with fresh fruits.

TABLE OF CONTENTS